BAD TASTE BIRTHDAY BOOK

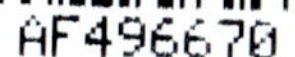

"Happy Birthd...

py Birthday..Happy Birthday...Happy Birthday..."

"*I know it's dead, but it was the only one they had left*"

HAPPY BIRTHDAY

"Nine today eh...looks old for his age doesn't he?"

"There's a clever girl. Mummy will just go and get the first aid kit then we'll cut the cake"

JUNIOR CHEMISTRY
JUNIOR
CHEMISTRY
SET
HAPPY
BIRTHDAY

"Cor, thanks Mum, thanks Dad, just what I wanted"

"I think now he's come of age the lazy sod should come out of there"

"You bastard...it was her Birthday today"

"Right...where's the Birthday boy?"

"As it's your Birthday I thought a 21 gun squad would be a nice touch"

"Happy Birthday to you – Happy Birthday to you..."

HAPPY BIRTHDAY
RON

"Well...there goes another one...how the years fly"

"Good Morning. How would you like to press my Birthday suit?"

"No peeping...Happy Birthday"

"Happy Birthday my dear – it's just a little something"

"Happy Birthday Butch"

"Here comes his big Birthday surprise...a Killergram"

"Happy Birthday Colin"

"Oh alright, as it's your Birthday, but hurry up, I've just got to an interesting bit"

"Ironic isn't it?...dying on your Birthday"

"For me!! What is it?"

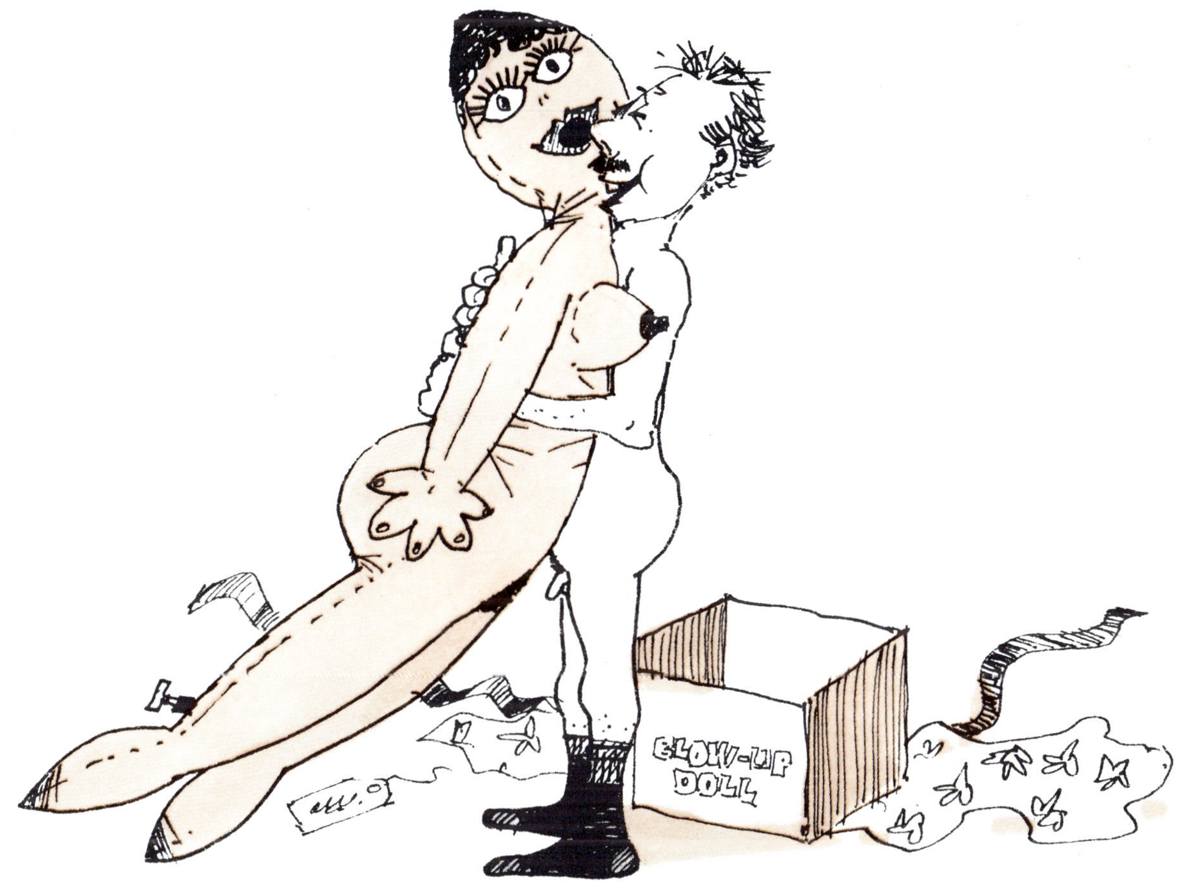

"Happy Birthday to me. Thank you, it's just what I've always wanted"

"It's lovely Herbert – just what I've always wanted"

"*Right!...close your eyes – open your mouth – Happy Birthday*"

"Hello Birthday boy – come to get your present?"

"Surprise! Surprise! Happy Hundred to Gran, Happy Hundred to Gran..

Happy Hundred to...?"